Written by Charis Mather

# BELFAST

Capitals of the UK

**BookLife PUBLISHING**

©2024
BookLife Publishing Ltd.
King's Lynn, Norfolk
PE30 4LS, UK

All rights reserved.
Printed in India.

A catalogue record for this book is available from the British Library.

ISBN: 978-1-80505-609-6

**Written by:**
Charis Mather

**Edited by:**
Noah Leatherland

**Designed by:**
Amelia Harris

*All facts, statistics, web addresses and URLs in this book were verified as valid and accurate at time of writing. No responsibility for any changes to external websites or references can be accepted by either the author or publisher.*

### Image Credits

All images are courtesy of Shutterstock.com, unless otherwise specified. With thanks to Getty Images, Thinkstock Photo and iStockphoto. Cover – Kite_rin, Serg Zastavkin, Konmac, Nahlik, dotmiller1986. Recurring images – Liliana Danila, Natasha Pankina, Voin_Sveta, ArtMari. 2–3 – Liliana Danila, Nick Fox. 4–5 – James Kennedy NI, Maxger. 6–7 – VVlasovs, okili77, Kalinin Ilya. 8–9 – National Library of Ireland on The Commons via Wikimedia Commons, Robert Welch, Public domain, via Wikimedia Commons. 10–11 – gabo, Attila Nagy toscana, Anton_Ivanov, meunierd. 12–13 – dotmiller1986, VanderWolf Images, Irina Wilhauk, British Museum, Public domain, via Wikimedia Commons. 14–15 – Irina Wilhauk, Nahlik. 16–17 – Maciek Grabowicz, Henryk Sadura, Vectorcarrot. 18–19 – stenic56, William Barton, IXIES. 20–21 – Ivan maguire, No machine-readable author provided. Miossec assumed (based on copyright claims), CC BY-SA 3.0 via Wikimedia Commons. 22–23 – Dignity100, iPlantsman, Alexey Fedorenko.

# CONTENTS

| | |
|---|---|
| Page 4 | Welcome to Belfast! |
| Page 6 | My Capital, My Country |
| Page 8 | Belfast Back Then |
| Page 10 | Shipyard Structures |
| Page 12 | Monuments to Remember |
| Page 14 | Places from the Past |
| Page 16 | Beautiful Belfast |
| Page 18 | Shopping in the City |
| Page 20 | City of Culture |
| Page 22 | Only in Belfast |
| Page 24 | Glossary and Index |

Words that look like <u>this</u> can be found in the glossary on page 24.

# Welcome to Belfast!

Belfast is a fantastic city, and I love living here. It can get quite busy in some places, but there are also plenty of beautiful <u>natural</u> areas that you can visit for a bit of quiet.

I love taking photos of all the interesting places in this city. I use these photos to share my favourite places in Belfast with my friends who have never been before.

# My Capital, My Country

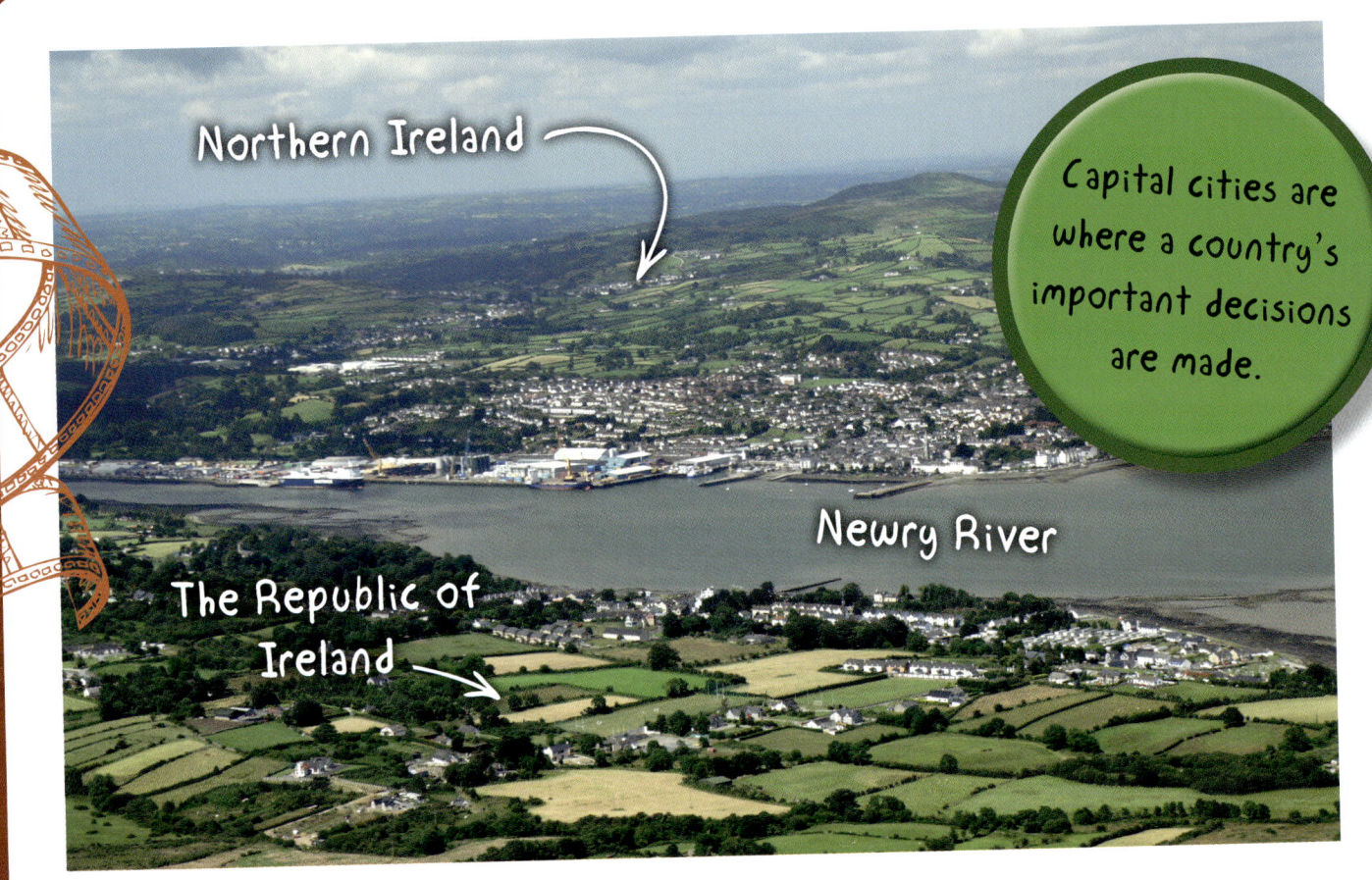

Capital cities are where a country's important decisions are made.

Belfast is the capital city of Northern Ireland. Northern Ireland shares an island with the Republic of Ireland, but they are completely different countries. Belfast is on Northern Ireland's northern <u>coast</u>.

Lots of people do not realise that Northern Ireland is part of the United Kingdom, which includes England, Scotland and Wales. However, Northern Ireland has its own important historical and <u>cultural</u> background.

Scotland

Northern Ireland

England

Belfast

Wales

The United Kingdom is often called the UK.

# Belfast Back Then

Over the years, Belfast has been known for a few different <u>industries</u>. Hundreds of years ago, it had a huge part in making a kind of cloth called linen. Belfast was nicknamed Linenopolis because of this.

Machines making linen in Belfast more than a hundred years ago

Belfast also became known for its shipbuilding, which helped make the city known around the world. There are a lot of <u>landmarks</u> in Belfast to remind you of this.

A ship being built in Belfast

# Shipyard Structures

Belfast's shipbuilding areas, called shipyards, look a bit different today. There are two famous yellow cranes in one of these shipyards. These cranes are named after Samson and Goliath, two very strong men.

**One of the most famous ships in the world, the *Titanic*, was built in Belfast.**

The Titanic

A museum about the Titanic in the Titanic Quarter

**Although the *Titanic* sank on its first journey, you can find out about its story in the city's Titanic Quarter.**

# Monuments to Remember

One of Belfast's most interesting <u>monuments</u> is a big fish statue. If you look closely at the Big Fish, you might notice that it is covered in information about Belfast's history.

The monument is based on an old Irish story about a <u>wise</u> salmon.

Another well-known monument is the **Albert Memorial Clock**. The clock tower does not stand completely straight because it was built on soft land. It is sometimes compared to Italy's famous leaning tower for that reason.

The Albert Memorial Clock is named after Queen Victoria's husband.

Prince Albert, Queen Victoria's husband

# Places from the Past

St Anne's Cathedral is a church that has been around for over a hundred years. It was built around another church building that was there before Belfast was even a proper city.

*Religion has had a huge part in Northern Ireland's history.*

St Anne's Cathedral

Belfast Castle

Over the years, there have been a few castles in Belfast. The oldest ones do not exist anymore. The one you can see now is on Cave Hill. It was built in 1862.

# Beautiful Belfast

Cave Hill has a great view over Belfast. You can also see it from many places in the city. Cave Hill gets its name from five caves on the side of its high <u>cliff</u> walls.

Cave Hill

Belfast's Botanic Gardens are near the River Lagan, which runs through the city. Here, lots of different kinds of plants are grown inside warm greenhouses. The Botanic Gardens also have a large rose garden.

# Shopping in the City

One of the activities that you might enjoy in Belfast is shopping. Belfast has had a Friday market day for more than 400 years.

Many people shop at St George's Market every week.

The Belfast City Hall and Christmas Market

In November and December, the area around Belfast's City Hall is usually turned into a Christmas market. The lights and decorations bring many people here to do their Christmas shopping.

# City of Culture

There are reminders of Belfast's culture and history all around the city. You can find many buildings that have artwork painted on them.

There are many pieces of art celebrating famous Northern Irish author, C.S. Lewis.

Art of C.S. Lewis and some of his famous children's story characters

Once a year, many people in Northern Ireland celebrate St Patrick's Day. St Patrick was an important person in this country's history. In Belfast, there is usually a <u>parade</u> in the streets.

Drummers taking part in Belfast's St Patrick's Day parade

# Only in Belfast

Crumlin Road Gaol

Belfast is a one-of-a-kind city. I have shown you some of my favourite spots, but there are many more fantastic places that you can discover for yourself!

Ulster Museum

Now you know what there is to see in Belfast, you know what to look forward to when you visit. Which places would you like to take your own pictures of?

23

# Glossary

| | |
|---|---|
| cliff | the high, steep side of a mountain or area of land |
| coast | where the land meets the sea |
| cultural | to do with the traditions, ideas and ways of life of a group of people |
| industries | types of activities and business |
| landmarks | places or buildings that are easily recognised |
| monuments | structures that are built to remember people or important events in the past |
| natural | found in nature and not made by people |
| parade | when people walk or dance down a street with others watching |
| religion | a system of faith and worship, especially to do with a god or gods |
| wise | clever and thoughtful |

castles 15
churches 14
cloth 8
coasts 6
gardens 17

hills 15–16
markets 18–19
ships 9–11
statues 12
Titanic, the 11